PICTURE
POST
IDOLS

Jon Savage has written on entertainment and popular culture for *The Observer*, *The Sunday Times*, *New Society*, *Melody Maker*, *The Face* and *Time Out*. His previous books are the official biography of The Kinks (1984) and *England's Dreaming: Sex Pistols and Punk Rock* (1991).

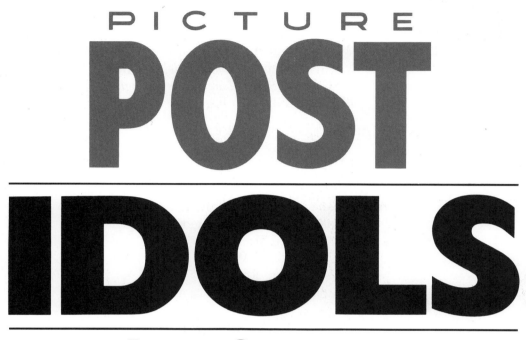

PICTURE
POST
IDOLS

Jon Savage

**TIGER BOOKS INTERNATIONAL
LONDON**

Front cover left to right:
First row: *Marlon Brando, David Niven, Elizabeth Taylor,*
Frankie Howerd, Joan Collins; Second row: *Tony Hancock, Elvis*
Presley, Alma Cogan, Tommy Steele, Richard Attenborough;
Third row: *James Dean, Marlene Dietrich, Vivien Leigh, Peter*
Sellers, Marilyn Monroe; Fourth row: *Alec Guinness, Noel*
Coward, Laurence Olivier, Veronica Lake, Louis Armstrong;
Fifth row: *Charlie Chaplin, Sophia Loren Arthur English,*
Bill Haley, Humphrey Bogart.

Back cover: *Charlie Chaplin and Buster Keaton in* Limelight

This edition published in 1994 by
Tiger Books International PLC, London

First published in Great Britain in 1991
by Collins & Brown Limited
London House
Great Eastern Wharf
Parkgate Road
London SW11 4NQ

A CIP catalogue record for this book
is available from the British Library

ISBN 1-85501-586-2

Conceived, edited and designed by Collins & Brown Limited

Editorial Director: Gabrielle Townsend
Editor: Sarah Hoggett
Picture Researcher: Frances Abraham
Art Director: Roger Bristow
Designed by: Gail Jones

Filmset by Servis Filmsetting Ltd, Manchester
Reproduction by Daylight, Singapore
Printed and bound in CHINA

Half title page: *Excited fans wait for*
Liberace after his début in Britain at the
London Palladium

Title page: *The classic glamour shot –*
Marilyn Monroe in Bus Stop

Contents

6
Introduction

10
Pin-ups and Propaganda
1938–1945

48
The 'Austerity Binge'
1945–1953

90
Sex, TV and Rock 'n' Roll
1953–1957

144
Acknowledgements

INTRODUCTION

Picture Post's attitude to idols was contradictory. From its inception in 1938, when Hollywood glamour was at its pre-war height, the magazine consciously set out to avoid the stylized studio shot or film still: as a 1942 editorial had it, 'film stills are photography at its most antiquated'. The typical Picture Post story on a famous actor, film star or pop performer did not portray a glamorous ideal, but rather placed the subject in a familiar world the readers could recognize and identify with.

On the other hand, like any magazine today, Picture Post needed a strong idol quotient to attract the reader. Commercial reality dictated that the magazine should contain glamour: 30 million cinema tickets were sold in Britain during the Blitz, mainly for American films. Despite a flourishing British film industry, it was Americans like Cary Grant, Veronica Lake or Betty Grable – or transplanted Brits like Vivien Leigh – who were the real idols of the day: untouchable, superhuman, almost perfect.

Lack of access to these stars was compounded by wartime restrictions on travel: it wasn't until 1951 that Picture Post visited Hollywood. When the first American performers began to venture to the UK in 1944, Picture Post was there to cover them as well. Until then, it relied on film stills and what became called 'pin-up girl shots': many Picture Post covers from this period feature American models with not many clothes on.

This mixture of canny populism and high-mindedness served Picture Post well during the war and immediate post-war years. As the magazine moved, however, from the 'Atom Age' into the 'Elizabethan Age' – between 1945 and 1953 – the mood of the country changed. The real winner of the Second World War was not England but America, and by 1948, England had become in thrall to the American way of life.

Right: *Vivien Leigh, 1938.*

Below: *A cinema queue in Piccadilly, 1953.*

Consumerism was the spearhead of this American takeover, embodied in the presence of the American GIs who had begun to land in Europe in January 1942. To the British, hamstrung by rationing and the austerity ethic, American products from films to nylons were the vanguard of a new way of life, in which, after the privations of war, prosperity for all was not to be scorned as materialistic but was a worthy human ideal.

America was the dream land for many Britons in those drab post-war years. American films were substitutes for transatlantic travel, picture windows looking out on fantastic scenes. The regular influx of American popular entertainers in the post-war years marked out a new emotional map of increased hysteria and sexuality, from the first regular appearances of jazz singers, to early 50's crooners like Johnny Ray, to the rock'n'roll stars who came in just at *Picture Post*'s demise.

Adolescents and children – a new generation with, for the first time, their own fashions and a new mould of heroes to idolize – were those most affected. After the war, as crime levels doubled, a new phrase entered the English vocabulary: the juvenile delinquent. This phrase was an importation from America, and it seemed to many people, including the editors and readers of *Picture Post*, that Britain's increasing reliance on, or domination by, America was a double-edged sword.

This tension is one of the storylines which underpins *Picture Post* in the 1950s: it is between an idealized and archaic Englishness and the increasing, if disturbing, freedom coming from America; between the Edwardian revivalism of 1951's Festival of Britain and the increasing lawlessness of spivs, cosh boys and teddy boys; between the wartime ethic of reform and solidarity and

the growing pressure for variety in consumer products.

In this, the single most powerful national event in the post-war years was the coronation of Queen Elizabeth II in June 1953. Although it succeeded in maintaining English tradition and the illusion of permanence, it also delivered England into the hands of television. Watched by 20 million (just under half the population of Britain), the coronation boosted sales of TV sets from 2 million in 1951 to 9 million in 1956 – about 95 per cent of the European total. Britain now found itself the European spearhead of American values.

The apparatus of modern society was now firmly in place: commercial TV, hire purchase, supermarkets and pop culture. From the cosy certainties of stars like Gracie Fields to the hysterical rock'n'roll star of today is a long road. Identified with a wartime and post-war era of social concern, *Picture Post* was now out of time: the magazine finally closed in July 1957, the advent of commercial television being cited as one of the principal reasons for its downfall.

The all-pervading influence of American values and fashions, epitomizing a more carefree way of life, could be seen in the immense popularity of jazz. Left: *dancing in a Newcastle Jazz club;* Below: *Nat King Cole.*

PIN-UPS AND PROPAGANDA
1938–1945

The first *Picture Post* story on popular culture started as the magazine meant to go on: concentrating on stars ran against the editors' 'conviction that the lives of ordinary people could be rewarding to curiosity'. In 1938, the craze was for a song and associated dance called 'The Lambeth Walk'- rather than concentrate on the performers of this song, *Picture Post* went down into Lambeth, then as now one of London's more deprived boroughs, using the song to expose severe social conditions.

Other early innovations were stories about the hard work that went into the creation of glamour or performance: the backstage life of a Windmill girl ('A glamour girl's day', October 1938), or the making of a hit ('Birth of a dance craze', January 1939). *Picture Post* did do star features, but in the early days these tended to be about such warm but homely (such was the domestic climate then) performers like Gracie Fields, the Crazy Gang or Leslie Henson.

Wartime restrictions on travel meant that *Picture Post* was only able to show many of the stars of the day in film stills, but the magazine's crusading approach meant that many of the greatest films of the day, including *Gone with The Wind*, went ignored in favour of domestic stars like Max Miller or Noel Coward who epitomized a sense of community and solidarity.

In the early days of the war, all cinemas, dance halls and theatres were shut down as a bombing risk: the radio was the only medium left. (The fledgling TV service was shut down in August

Left: *Cheeky chappie Max Miller, at the Grosvenor House Hotel, 1938. In the era of the stand-up comedian, Max Miller was king of the boards with his hair-trigger, salacious patter.*

1938.) By early 1940, these public places were opened again and were packed as never before: the lavish escapism of Hollywood movies was especially popular. A film like *Gone with the Wind*, although set in the American Civil War, reflected the worries of the English at war in a highly stylized, glossy manner.

Reflecting a mood similar to that of popular songs like 'Lili Marlene' or 'That Lovely Weekend', romances were perennially popular, from *Gone with the Wind* to 1941's *49th Parallel*, starring the recently married Laurence Olivier and Vivien Leigh, to the darker *Casablanca*, starring Ingrid Bergman and Humphrey Bogart. This was also the heyday of Disney, *Bambi* and *Fantasia* being two of his best-known cartoons.

The British film industry could not compete with this injection of glamour. Most films from this period fall into one of three categories: the historical drama, heavy on set design and the evocation of nostalgia (rather like the series still pumped out by the big ITV companies) – examples include 1940's *Disraeli* or Olivier's famous 1944 *Henry V*; sheer

Above*: Laurence Olivier in his 1944 film* Henry V. *Olivier also directed the film.*

Below*: The Crazy Gang.*

Opposite*: Dooley Wilson sings 'As Time Goes By' to Humphrey Bogart and Ingrid Bergman in* Casablanca.

escapist whimsy, like Coward's brilliant *Blithe Spirit*; or war drama, like 1942's popular *One of our Aircraft is Missing*.

It was not only American plots but American flesh that was popular. This was the age of the more sexually aggressive starlet, like Veronica Lake, whose hairstyle set a fashion trend, or Betty Grable, whose 'million-dollar legs' made her the forces' most popular pin-up, irrespective of her acting abilities. *Picture Post* was forced to accede to popular demand, and from 1942 on began using 'pin-up girl' shots from America by photographers like Andre De Dienes, later famous for taking the first glamour shots of Marilyn Monroe. These became a feature in themselves in an October 1943 spread: 'What Makes a Pin-up Girl? Soldiers choose their favourites'.

Popular music from the time expressed a similarly strong sexuality: swing was all the rage in the dance halls and sentimental love ballads dominated the radio. The most successful bands, like Glenn Miller's, balanced this mix between sensuality and sentiment. Large dance bands ruled the dance halls and clubs, although the featured vocalist was coming up fast, with the success of 'crooners' like Bing Crosby – whom *Picture Post* photographed on his 1944 visit to the UK.

In New York, 30,000 bobbysoxers were rioting for Frank Sinatra; in the UK, the most popular singer of the period was the rather more demure Vera Lynn: boosted by a radio link-up show called *Sincerely Yours*, 'the forces' sweetheart' caught the mood with songs like 'Faithful for Ever' and the infamous 'We'll Meet Again'. Another of the war's biggest hits was Bing Crosby's perennial 'White Christmas', featured in the 1942 film *Holiday Inn*.

Many of these major names were photographed in *Picture Post*'s documentary style. This approach also led to features on classic films and theatre performances during this period – Richard Attenborough being dressed for the play of *Brighton Rock*, or Michael Redgrave making-up as MacHeath in *The Threepenny Opera*. There are also fine stories about the social locations of glamour – jazz fans in an early jazz club, a coloured serviceman's club – a hint of the changes to come.

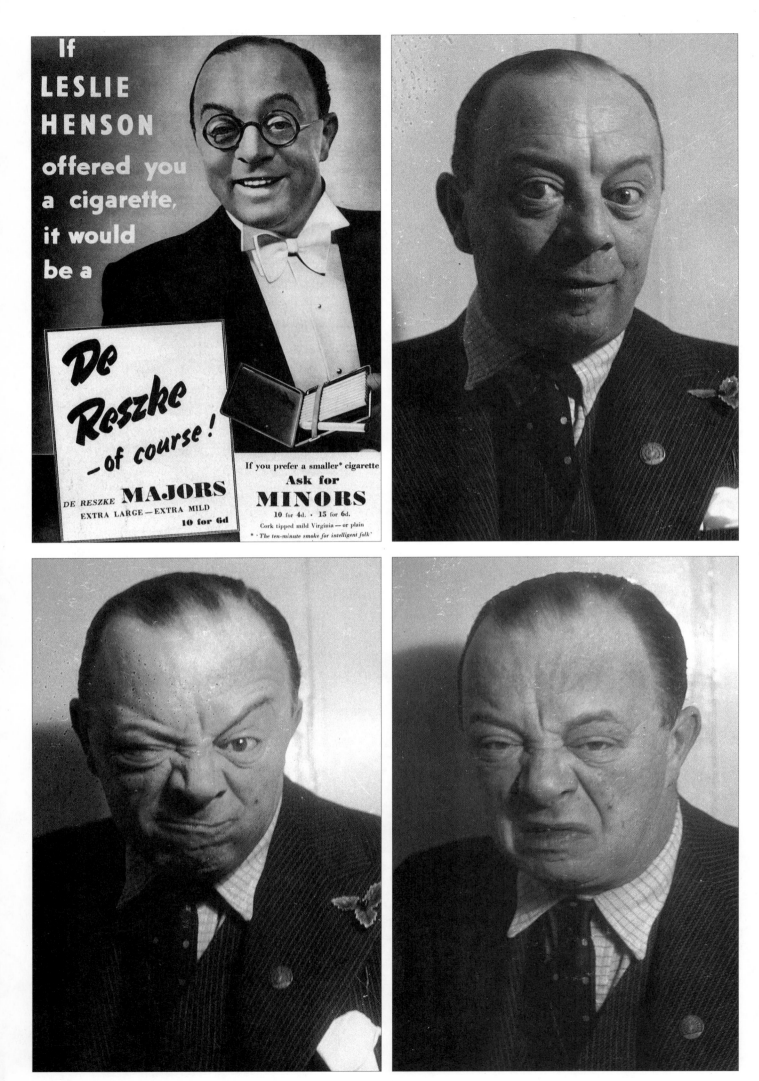

An early example of a creative Picture Post *layout in this January 1939 spread. Leslie Henson was a veteran variety performer who had been treading the boards since the First World War. His specialities – farce and musical comedy – made him the 1930s' equivalent of today's sitcom or soap opera star.*

Tommy Handley's ITMA – 'It's that man again'

A national obsession, ITMA's surreal style reflected the frustrations of a nation at war.

Above: *Tommy Handley, Fred Yule and Jack Train.*

Below: *Pictured at a 'script conference' in 1945 are Tommy Handley, Francis Worsley (BBC producer) and Ted Kavanagh (scriptwriter).*

Right: *As befits a national institution, Handley celebrates victory in May 1945 with 'Mrs Mopp' (Dorothy Summers). Several ITMA catchphrases – including Mrs Mopp's 'Shall I do yer now, sir?' – passed into the English language.*

Role models for a whole generation

Right: *British-born Freddie Bartholomew (right), pictured here with Micky Rooney in* A Yank at Eton *(1942), had shot to fame as David Copperfield in 1934.*

Far right: *Shirley Temple, in a more adult role (1942's* Kathleen*), inspired thousands of mothers to dress their daughters in her image.*

The stars did their bit for the war effort

Below: *Gracie Fields in a BBC studio, October 1939. Her down-to-earth comic songs and chatter made her one of the biggest home-grown stars of the 1930s.*

Right: *George Formby 'entertains a Battalion of the Buffs' with his trademark ukelele, France, March 1940.*

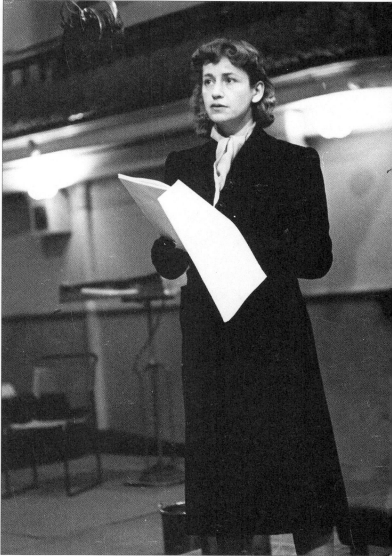

Speaking for Britain: David Niven (above), Peggy Ashcroft *(right),* J.B. Priestley *(below)* and Noel Coward *(left).*

Wartime films with a wartime setting

Above: *Clark Gable and Vivien Leigh in* Gone with the Wind. *Its lush production values, melodramatic storyline and American Civil War setting made it the most popular film of the war.*

Right: *Humphrey Bogart and Ingrid Bergman in Michael Curtiz's* Casablanca. *This 1942 film captured the prevailing mood of romance, danger and self-sacrifice.*

VERONICA LAKE
in Paramount Pictures

American stars provided some much-needed glamour to lift wartime spirits.

Opposite, top left: *Veronica Lake, America's 'new glamour starlet',* 1941. *Her 'peek-a-boo bang' hairstyle was much imitated.*

Opposite, top right: *Cary Grant in* 1942. *The debonair Archibald Leach (British-born Grant's real name) was one of Hollywood's biggest wartime stars, with films like* The Philadelphia Story *(*1940*)*, Talk of the Town *(*1942*) and* Arsenic and Old Lace *(*1944*).*

Opposite, bottom: *John Wayne in a typical pose in* 1942*'s* The Shepherd of the Hills.

Left: *Marlene Dietrich in* Manpower, 1941. *'Miss Legs', as the GIs called her, was a sensation when she travelled around the USA on wartime concert tours and hospital visits.*

Wartime cinema in the UK was dominated by period drama or out-and-out propaganda. Above: *John Mills and Noel Coward in 1943's* In Which We Serve. Left: *A scene from* One of Our Aircraft is Missing, *one of 1942's most successful English films.*

Picture Post *often went behind the scenes rather than showing film stills.* Top right: *Leslie Howard's first day at work on his film* Pimpernel Smith, *February 1941.* Centre right: *Leslie Arliss directing Margaret Lockwood and Michael Rennie in the* Wicked Lady, *1945.* Bottom right: *The cast of 1940's* Disraeli *undergoing the rigours of wartime, in costumes typical of this period's nostalgia.*

Backstage

Michael Redgrave (above) *and Ralph Richardson*
(right) *preparing to tread the boards.*

Star-crossed lovers . . .

The 1940 marriage of a Gone with the Wind star and England's foremost young actor made Vivien Leigh and Laurence Olivier the most celebrated couple of the day, a status recognized by an April 1941 Picture Post cover story, 'The Oliviers at Home'. The lovers are pictured (below) on stage in Romeo and Juliet in 1940 and (right) at a press conference in January 1941.

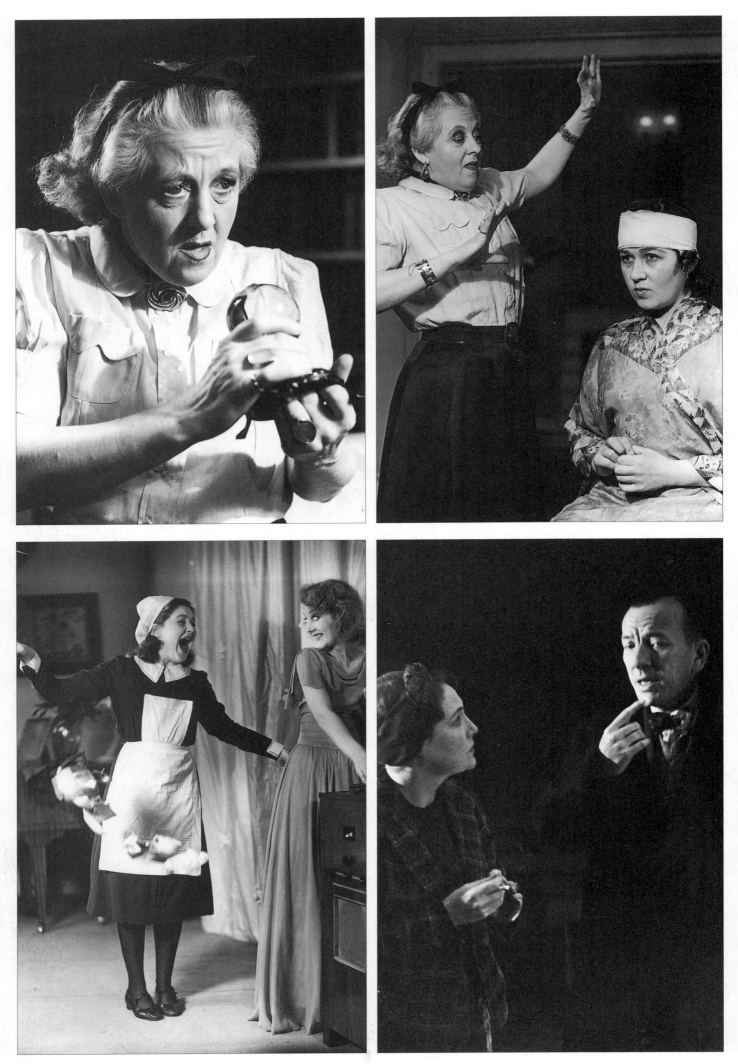

34

Blithe Spirit

Noel Coward's Blithe Spirit*: 'a mixture of slapstick, satire and wit to make us forget our troubles', said* Picture Post. *In scenes from rehearsal: Noel Coward (below); Margaret Rutherford as Madame Arcati* (top left)*; Margaret Rutherford with Ruth Reeves as Edith (top right); Noel Coward drills Fay Compton as Ruth (bottom right); Ruth Reeves with Kay Hammond as Elvira (bottom left).*

The English gangster play that became a classic

Graham Greene's Brighton Rock, 'a tough and sordid story of the underworld', starred Hermione Baddeley, Dulcie Gray and the 19-year-old Richard Attenborough, playing 'one of the most difficult parts in current plays – the vicious, inhuman, petty gangster, Pinkie'.

Going to a dance meant live music . . .

Left: *Henry Hall, April 1944.* Above: *Ivy Benson fronts her All-Girl Orchestra,* *October 1942.* Below: *Lou Praeger at the Hammersmith Palais,* February 1945.

Pin-up girls

The 'pin-up girl', tacked up in army billets or painted on the side of American bombers, was a phenomenon of the war.

Far right: *The most popular was Hollywood's Betty Grable, whose 1939 film,* Million Dollar Legs, *said it all.*

Right: *Rather more demure was Vera Lynn, pictured here in a May 1945 Victory Broadcast. She became irrevocably linked with the war through songs like 'We'll Meet Again' and 'The White Cliffs of Dover'.*

In the mood

Glenn Miller fronting the AEF band in
1944. The unsolved mystery surrounding his
death on 15 December 1944 helped to
enshrine him in myth.

The Stage Door Canteen *opens in London, September 1944*

This revue-style show was one of the first opportunities to see American stars in wartime England. Left: *Bing Crosby in full flight. His biggest hit, 'White Christmas', was featured in 1942's* Holiday Inn. *Far left: Crosby's* Holiday Inn *co-star, Fred Astaire, 'improvises a boogy-woogy dance in his outdoor shoes'.* Below: *Long-time Coward colleague, Bea Lillie, returns to the UK to sing.*

Cheering the troops

Left: *The Andrews Sisters, Maxene, Patty and Laverne.* Below: *As peace broke out fellow American singer Josephine Baker, based in Paris, was 'giving the soldiers a victory song'.*

THE 'AUSTERITY BINGE'

1945–1953

Everything was changing after the war years, as post-war austerity gave way to premonitions of a more prosperous, but troubled, future. A new generation of radio comedians was coming up, with a harsher, more fractured style – like the Goons, whom *Picture Post* caught in an early, 1951 feature. The wholesome sexuality of film stars like Betty Grable was replaced by the more provocative sexiness of Marilyn Monroe, or the brooding looks of Montgomery Clift.

Just as colour starts to bleed into the inside of *Picture Post* during 1947 (by 1952, colour covers are routine) Britain slowly got back to normal after six years of war. The process was gradual, and painful. Rationing lasted until well into the Fifties: compared to the images of plenty flooding in from America, Britain had little to offer. For many, it was like looking through a shop window at all things that they could not touch.

This sense of longing gives this period its confused, stressed flavour – the 'Austerity Binge'. Under every public exhortation to save resources lay hundreds of cinema seats sold: the cinemas were full after the war as never before, as the public flocked to American films, romances, adventures, westerns. There was mass emigration, particularly among young people, to the remains of the Commonwealth: Rhodesia, Australia, Canada, New Zealand.

While American films charted the map of the public's secret desires – from the conventional glamour of Rita Hayworth to the twisted

Left: *Rita Hayworth, in London for the world premiere of* Down to Earth *(1947):* '*Would the crowds who waited in vain to feast their eyes on Rita Hayworth have recognised her if they'd seen her?' asked* Picture Post.

neuroticism of new youth culture idols like Marlon Brando and Montgomery Clift – British films were full of what *they* wanted you to think. Whimsy, a pumped-up sense of community and nostalgia for an idealized Edwardian past plagued domestic films: only the best, like *It Always Rains on Sundays* or David Lean's *Oliver Twist* addressed the mood of the present.

This Edwardian hankering found its expression in novels, paintings and the 1951 Festival of Britain: the public event that was to set the mood for Britain's post-war future. A golden age of theatre, with actors like John Gielgud, Alec Guinness, Ralph Richardson and Laurence Olivier, established a new English classical tradition which would last for another forty years.

With the post-war relaxations on travel – ads for foreign travel start to appear after 1946 – Britain was host to a wider selection of American singers and groups than it had before, from the black vocal styles of the Inkspots to jazz singers like Lena Horne. The music hall was in retreat but the dance hall – as immortalized in Diana Dors' 1950 film of that name – was booming. Just as in film, the wartime idols were replaced by new, more neurotic performers, most notably Johnny Ray, who wore a hearing aid on stage and twisted himself into paroxysms of tears.

Behind all this was the creeping fear of Americanization, which seemed sometimes like a direct threat to the humane, if cosy life offered by the British fantasy factory; Orwell sounded the

Above right: *John Gielgud and Peggy Ashcroft, two of the leading lights of British theatre, in* A Midsummer Night's Dream *(1945)*.

Right: *Lena Horne sings the blues at the London Palladium in 1950. Lena Horne also appeared in several films, including the spectacular* Ziegfeld Follies *which featured such legends in their own lifetime as Fred Astaire, Gene Kelly and Judy Garland.*

warning in his 1944 essay, *No Orchids for Miss Blandish*. At the same time as it freely indulged in the fruits of the US media, *Picture Post* was not immune to a spot of Yank-bashing. Americanization (as well as a crude Freudianism: the kids' fathers were away in the war) was used to explain a puzzling phenomenon: the rise in juvenile delinquency.

As the consumer boom began to take off in the early fifties, these fears hit the headlines in a 'moral panic'. The case of Craig and Bentley, in which a policeman was shot dead, gripped the nation in lurid headlines. Bentley's execution in February 1953 – a miscarriage of justice highlighted in the 1991 film, *Let 'Em Have It* –

coincided with the release of the first British juvenile delinquency film proper, *Cosh Boy*. *Picture Post* ran a large spread on it.

In this low-budget film, the young, petty criminals of the time (three years earlier, they would have been called spivs, a year later, they'd be called Edwardians) ape American accents as they rob old ladies of their handbags. The film's plotline and moral are ludicrous, but this feature inaugurated *Picture Post*'s coverage of a phenomenon that would provide much copy over the last four years of its life: the teenager. The new Elizabethan age dawned: it was not quite what had been expected.

Below*: Googie Withers and Susan Shaw in* It Always Rains on Sundays. *This 1947 film about an escaped convict in the East End of London, which also starred Jack Warner, was widely praised for its realistic portrayal of London low life.*

Hollywood old and new

The inspired pairing of Humphrey Bogart and Katherine Hepburn (below) *made the claustrophobic* The African Queen *into one of 1952's big hits, while Gloria Swanson and Erich von Stroheim* (above) *overacted deliciously in Billy Wilder's* Sunset Boulevard *(1950). The new type of star was epitomized by Marlon Brando, seen* (right) *with Vivien Leigh in his 1952 film,* A Streetcar Named Desire.

When idols wore ties . . . archetypal Hollywood heroes

Opposite, top: *Douglas Fairbanks Jnr;* opposite, bottom: *James Mason;* top left: *Errol Flynn;* bottom left: *Humphrey Bogart.*

The Marx Brothers

The heyday of the Marx Brothers was over, but a UK visit was still worthy of coverage. In June 1949, Harpo and Chico came to play the London Palladium. Groucho, pictured (left) with his secretary, visited in July 1954: 'everyone was far keener to meet him than he was to meet them'.

CC-8
P-456

Varieties of British leading men

A studio portrait of Richard Todd (left) in the 1950 film, Portrait of Clare. *Todd was very popular in the early 1950s, contributing to what writer Andy Medhurst has called 'the hegemony of the tweed jacket' in male imagery. Another studio portrait of a favourite leading man, Rex Harrison (below left). Recent films then included* Blithe Spirit *(1945) and* Unfaithfully Yours *(1948). Dirk Bogarde (opposite) was one of the few actors to break out of this mould, with roles like the boy gangster in* The Blue Lamp *(1950). He is seen here co-starring with Jon Whiteley in* Hunted *(1952).*

Silent stars make a comeback

Previous page: *Charlie Chaplin gets his silent-film contemporary Buster Keaton out of an unhappy retirement for* Limelight *in October 1952.*

Literary classics on screen
Opposite, top: *Alec Guinness (Herbert Pocket) and John Mills (Pip) in* Great Expectations, *one of 1947's most popular films.* Opposite, bottom: *Alec Guinness and David Lean on the set of Lean's 1948* Oliver Twist, *its dark melodrama vividly reflecting England's post-war gloom. Anthony Asquith's 1952 adaptation of* The Importance of Being Earnest: *Margaret Rutherford as Miss Prism* (above right), *Edith Evans as Lady Bracknell* (left), *and Michael Denison as Algernon Moncrieff* (above left).

Ealing Studios

Ealing Studios was in a late flowering with a series of comedies which mocked post-war austerity. In December 1951, Picture Post did a long feature about the 'Ealing Studios Tradition'. Featured were 1948's Passport to Pimlico *(top right and bottom right),* Whisky Galore *(1948) (centre right), and* The Lavender Hill Mob *(1954) (below).*

Cosh Boy

A 1953 film, 'cheaply made and artistically undistinguished', about London's juvenile delinquents.

Top left: *James Kenney as gang-leader Roy Walsh and Ian Whittaker as his accomplice Alfie Collins.*

Centre left: *16-year-olds deliver their judgement. 'Making love to Joan Collins is not worth the risk of going to prison', said one.*

Bottom left: *Joan Collins with Kenney in this, her second film.*

Opposite: *Ex-con Danny Hughes faces the poster for the film 'in which he could have played the real-life lead'.*

Home-grown talent

Above: *Diana Dors on a 'day trip to Boulogne',
August 1950. Dors was currently appearing in the
cinemas in* Dance Hall. *Publicity shots of two new
stars:* Liz Taylor (right) *and Joan Collins* (below).

Theatrical legends in the making

The Fifties were a golden age for the development of a great theatrical tradition.

Above left: Peter Ustinov making up.

Above: John Gielgud preparing for a quick change.

Left: Alec Guinness and Yvonne De Carlo practise the mamba.

Right: Michael Redgrave being fitted for a new stage wig.

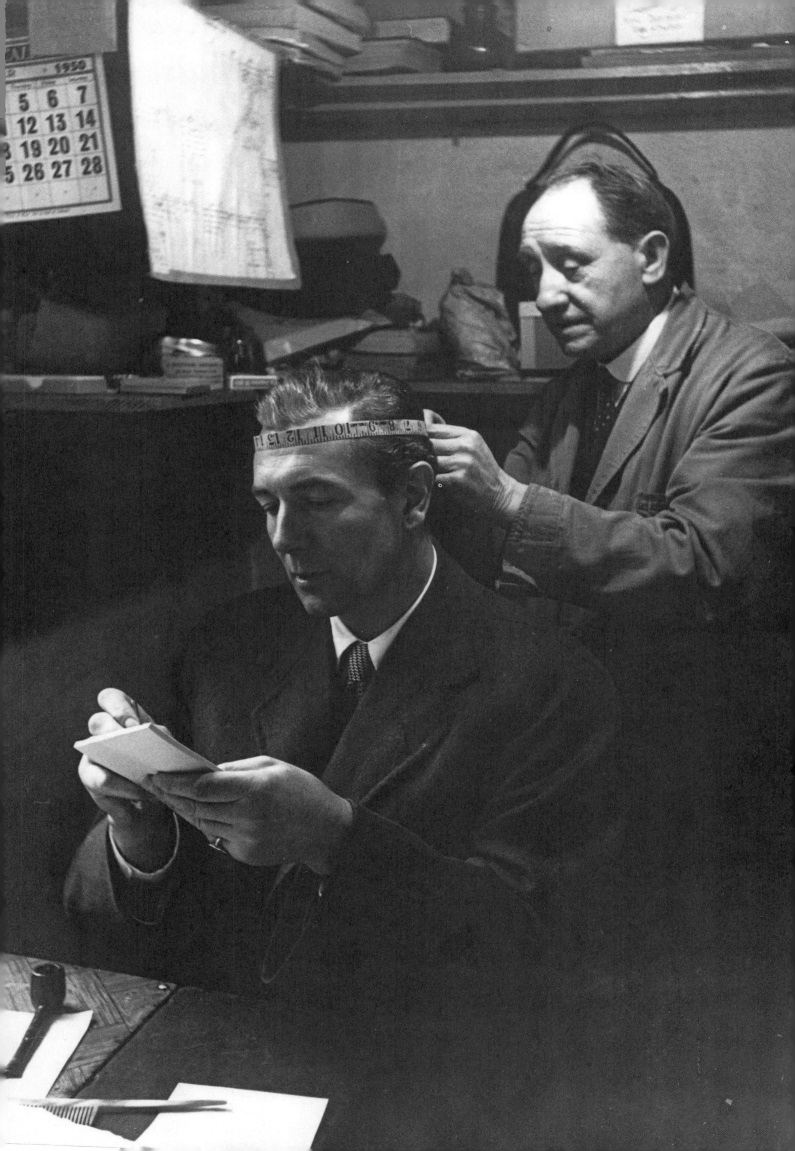

The big American musicals

In the early Fifties the musical was, almost by definition, American. No one else could rival their tunes, their dancers, their sheer vitality. Below: Seven Brides for Seven Brothers *with Howard Keel and Jane Powell;* top right: *acrobatics in Cole Porter's* Kiss Me Kate; bottom right: *Gene Kelly in* Singin' in the Rain.

Britain's favourite American comedian

The arrival of Danny Kaye for the Royal Command
Performance was big news in November 1948, as was
still any UK visit by an American star. Left: Danny
Kaye with UK comedian Sid Field. Top: Kaye was
a consummate performer: as one contemporary source
said, 'an astonishing success, who constantly, suddenly
and unplanned, does the unexpected'. Above: At the
Albert Hall with legendary classical pianist, Artur
Rubinstein.

The Inkspots come to London

*October 1946: the first UK visit of the most popular
black American vocal group of the Thirties and
Forties. Their best-known song was 'Whispering
Grass' (1940), whose troubled choruses help to propel
the song's title into the vernacular: 'Why do you
whisper, green grass? Why tell the trees what ain't so?
Whispering grass, the trees don't have to know'.*

A new jazz age

After the war, Soho dives like the Leicester Square Jazz Club were packed with teenagers, dancing to the hearty UK adaptation of New Orleans styles from the teens and twenties that was later marketed as Trad Jazz. Above: Blissed out on shandy and the sounds of Chris Barber, Mick Mulligan and their bands, April 1951.

Left: American music; American products. Top right: Humphrey Lyttelton in action at the Hammersmith Palais, April 1951.

Bottom right: 'A new jazz age' captured at the 100 Club, November 1949. Lurking behind these stories was the sensational spectre of drugs.

'The nabob of sob'

Johnny Ray, shown here in April 1953, rehearsing for a performance at the London Palladium, was the first new-style American pop star to visit England. Part native Indian, he began by singing R & B but hit his stride by making capital out of male vulnerability and emotional excess. His tortured performance of ballads like 'Cry' and 'The Little White Cloud That Cried' drove young, female audiences crazy.

Uncanned laughter . . .

Radio comedy programmes in the 1940s were often recorded in front of a live audience. Their stage experience stood radio stars like Norman Wisdom (top), Arthur English (centre) and Terry Thomas (bottom) in good stead.

'The Men You Laugh At'

Below: *In May 1952,* Picture Post *did a feature about the 'race for the still vacant crown of ITMA in the gang show business'. Among the comics featured was a young Frankie Howerd* (below), *then at the peak of his first success after 1950's revue,* Out of This World. Left: *Wilfred Pickles rehearses at a factory for* Have A Go, *May 1947. BBC offic als at the time noted that his 'unscripted social conscience' was 'an embarrassment'.*

The Goons

The modern sensibility – anarchic and absurd – arrives with the surreal humour of the Goons. Their early days are captured at the Grafton's Pub in Victoria (above, left to right): *Spike Milligan, Peter Sellers, Michael Bentine and Harry Secombe. The show is* Those Crazy People; *the Goons wanted it to be called* Junior Crazy Gang.

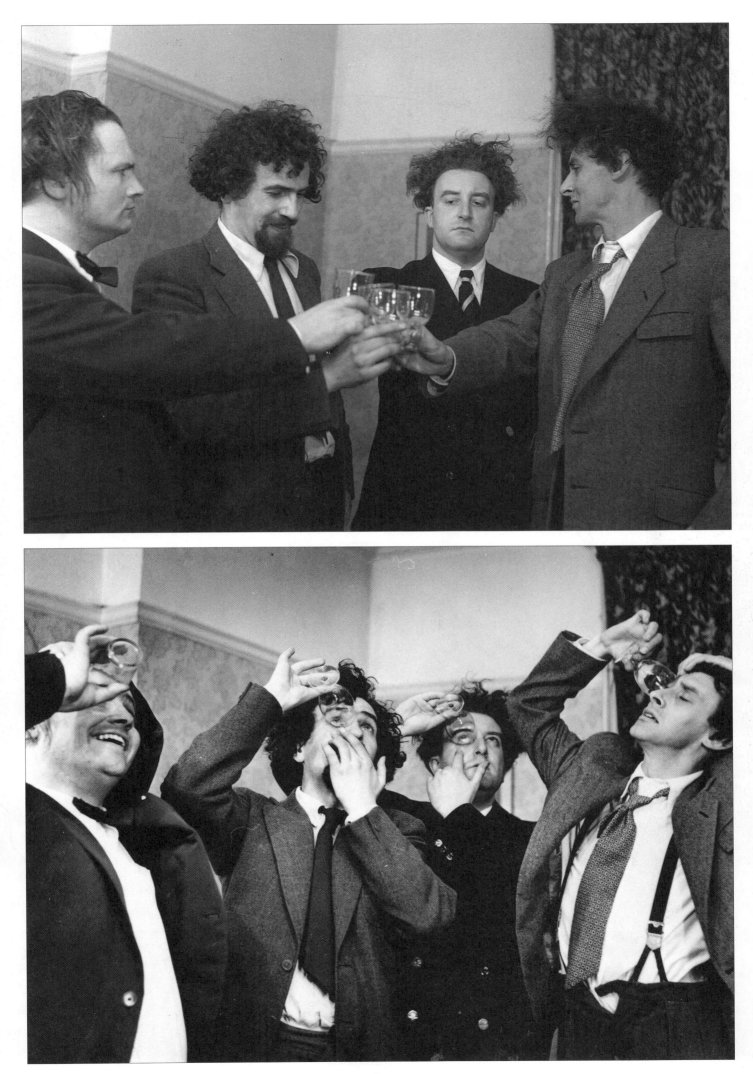

Royalty on TV

If television turned the Royal Family into superstars, it was they who established the universal appeal of TV. Below: TV cameras film the royal wedding in 1947. Top right: Richard Dimbleby practising his Coronation commentary before the ceremony. Centre right: *the Royal Family gathered on the balcony of Buckingham Palace. Bottom right:* the State Coach on *its way to Westminster Abbey.*

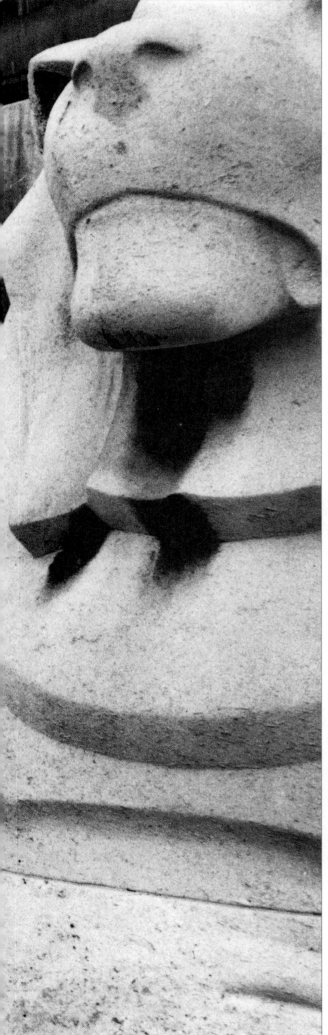

SEX, TV AND ROCK 'N' ROLL

1953-1957

We now tend to think of the Fifties as a golden age, secure and untroubled. Yet the idols parading through the pages of *Picture Post* during its last four years continue a darker, more blatant post-war trend: the exaggerated (and, as we now know, doomed) sexuality of Marilyn Monroe was reproduced in a dozen American and English starlets – Sabrina, Diana Dors, Yana, Jayne Mansfield. The avant-garde dissonance of modern jazz was replaced by the wild shrieks of the first rock'n'roll.

The American take-over of Britain's fantasy life was nearly complete, and nowhere was this truer than in the televizing of the monarchy. A *Picture Post* cover of late 1952 already talks about Princess Margaret as the 'TV Princess': when 20 million watched the Coronation in June 1953, it was clear that the much trumpeted Elizabethan age would be televized. *Picture Post* gallantly tried to keep abreast of trends, with TV covers, columns by luminaries like Gilbert Harding, and reportage of the start of ITV in September 1955.

Television poached audiences from both radio and cinema (especially domestic cinema – Ealing Studios closed down during this period) and further hastened the decline of the music hall. Many of the young comedians captured by *Picture Post* photographers during this period became household television names during the next twenty years: Eric Morecambe and Ernie Wise, Benny Hill, Tony Hancock, Frankie Howerd.

A new generation of film stars made the vaguely troubled persona of an idol like Montgomery Clift

Left: 'Alfred Hitchcock, master director and suspense spinner of the cinema, passes through London and pauses to pick out a few sinister scenes': the British Museum, January 1955.

seem passé. *Picture Post* dramatized the new choice in a typical headline: 'Brando or beefcake? Two fashions in heroes are in vogue in Hollywood, the gentle tough with a beautiful torso, or the broody, crazy mixed-up kid'. The likes of Jeff Chandler and Tony Curtis were contrasted with Marlon Brando, Paul Newman and James Dean.

Popular music, too, went through a major change at this time. Until 1956, the idols of the day were 'crooners', facsimiles of the big-band tradition established by Frank Sinatra and Bing Crosby before him. *Picture Post* gave generous feature space to these, and pre-war American jazzers visiting the UK for the first time since the war. Home-grown stars like Frankie Vaughan, Dickie Valentine and Alma Cogan were seen by *Picture Post* as maybe a bit much, but human: boys and girls next door. As minor star Edna Savage stated so eloquently, 'I suppose they like me because I'm like them'.

The new American imports disturbed such verities. Bill Haley, sedate by today's standards, created riots on his visit in February 1957, the first by an American rock'n'roller, while even Liberace ('the showman of television') created fan hysteria during his October 1956 visit. Neither, however, compared to the impact of Elvis Presley, whose 'Heartbreak Hotel' went into the Top Ten in the early summer of 1956. *Picture Post* celebrated this new phenomenon with an October cover which proclaimed: 'Elvis Presley – rock'n'roll arrives'.

In contrast to its previously subjective handling of such phenomena, *Picture Post* entered the Elizabethan age as a kind of tip-sheet. 'Has Italy succeeded in producing a new breed of girls?' asked a September 1954 headline, in response to the European exoticism of film stars like Sophia Loren and Gina Lollobrigida. The establishment of James Dean as a cult figure immediately after his premature death ensured massive coverage in *Picture Post* during 1956.

The combination of good quality colour printing and the heavy ratio of pictures to text could have ensured *Picture Post* a great future in this new pop age, but the magazine attempted to hold on to its previous constituency by heavy-handed attempts to analyse 'the Truth About Teenagers'. There was also an attempt to 'boy-next-door' the first English rock'n'roll star, Tommy Steele, in an echo of that first 'Lambeth Walk' story of 1938.

This was not what the teenagers themselves wanted to read about, nor their parents. Teens wanted hysteria, not homilies, and their parents could watch the truth about teenagers or anything else, should they have wished, on the documentary strands developed by the BBC and the new ITV. After almost two decades, in the course of which photo-journalism had become an accepted part of British magazine publishing, *Picture Post* foundered in a welter of cute animal pictures and non-stories.

Unreachable American idols versus a cosy homegrown hero: (left to right) *Elvis, Hancock and James Dean.*

The Big Band Sound

Clockwise from top right: *Dennis Lotis; Ted Heath with vocalist Kathy Lloyd; Edmundo Ros with the Ray Ellington Orchestra; Victor Silvester with* (centre) *his Television Dancing Club show; Mantovani.*

The flowering of British comedy, 1954–5

Clockwise from top left: Max Wall,
Stanley Baxter, Frankie Howerd, Eric
Morecambe and Ernie Wise, Arthur Askey.

Bluebell Girls

'Glamour' shots of women, whether pin-up girls or dancing troupes, were always a Picture Post *staple. Here Bert Hardy captures the Bluebell Girls in Paris, July 1955.*

Liberace

September 25, 1956: 'Liberace arrives in London. Crowds of fans were at Waterloo Station today to greet Liberace, idol of American television, who arrived on the Queen Mary boat train for his first visit to this country. The 35-year-old publicity-loving pianist, who is here for 11 days, was accompanied by his mother and his brother George.' Above: Liberace, mother Frances and candelabra: the Savoy Hotel.

**Fifties'
Heart-throbs**

*Tame and sedate
by today's pop-
star standards,
Alma Cogan
(opposite),
Dickie Valentine
(right) and
Edna Savage
(below) all
pulled in the
crowds.*

The Crooner

In the pre-rock'n'roll period, the pop idol was the big band singer – or, as some preferred to call them then, crooners. Left: Frank Sinatra in action during a July 1953 visit to Britain. Right: Frankie Laine, one of this period's biggest stars – his 'I Believe' topped the charts for 18 weeks in 1953 – at the Liverpool Empire in October 1954. Below: the home-grown Frankie Vaughan signing autographs, August 1954.

The Prince and the Showgirl

Below: *When Marilyn Monroe married Arthur Miller, the headline was 'Egghead weds Hourglass'. The actress (who later starred with Laurence Olivier in* The Prince and the Showgirl*) and the playwright are pictured here at the October 1956 Royal Film Performance.*

Right: *Real-life prince and showgirl, Prince Rainier of Monaco and* High Society *star Grace Kelly, married in April 1956, in the full glare of attention from the world's press and TV cameras.*

American glamour girls . . .

Clockwise from left: *Marilyn Monroe and Jane Russell in* Gentlemen Prefer Blondes; *Kim Novak, 1954; Ava Gardner, 1956; Jayne Mansfield, 1957.*

. . . and their British challengers

The British starlets of the period tended to ape the overstuffed glamour of their American counterparts. Above: Joan Collins 'returns from Hollywood', October 1955. Right: Diana Dors is hailed as 'Queen of Cannes', May 1956. Left: Sabrina, February 1956. 'A cult takes to culture,' said Picture Post. 'Sabrina worship has reached a new frenzy. But Sabrina, alias Norma Sykes of Blackpool, is not satisfied. A 40-inch bust is not enough. A girl must improve herself.'

Sexy stars from the continent
A powerful counterpoint to American glamour.
Clockwise from top left: *Zsa Zsa Gabor; Brigitte Bardot; Elsa Martinelli; Sophia Loren.*

Jazz enjoyed a heyday in the early to mid-Fifties, before the onslaught of rock'n'roll. Below: Peerless vocalist Billie Holiday makes her only visit to Britain, October 1954. Picture Post *shot her but didn't run the story.* Right: *Jazz on Tyneside at the 'Club Martinique'. 'The band . . . play Dixieland and jazz in the New Orleans manner.' April 1955.*

Overleaf: *Louis 'Satchmo' ('Satchelmouth') Armstrong was back in Britain in May 1956 after a quarter-century's absence. 'Even having to fight against the impossible acoustics of the Empress Hall, his breathtaking, irresistible virtuoso playing provokes a frenzied acclamation,' reported* Picture Post.

Left: 'Stan Kenton and his Orchestra are the first American band to tour Britain since 1934. Their music is the loudest jazz in the world, contemporary, ultra-modern style, full of dissonance and organised chaos.' March 1956.

Top right: 'Latest convert to the current 'Rock'n'roll' craze is American band leader, Lionel Hampton.' October 1956. Once an unknown vibraphone player, he started his jazz career with the Benny Goodman Quartet. Then he started his own large band and played good jazz, but rock'n'roll proved too great a temptation.

Bottom right: Louis Armstrong in May 1956 with Velma Middleton.

The Hollywood old guard, suave and sophisticated! Clockwise from top*: Yul Brynner; Gregory Peck; Robert Mitchum; and Douglas Fairbanks.*

The Method Actors

By the mid 1950s there was a new generation of intense, brooding 'method-acting' stars. Clockwise from top left: *Marlon Brando in* On the Waterfront, *1954; Montgomery Clift in De Sica's 1954* Indiscretion of an American Wife; *Rod Steiger, co-star of* On the Waterfront, *at Cannes in 1956.*

Overleaf: *The archetypal rebel image of the early 1950s: Marlon Brando in 1954's* The Wild One. *Although* Picture Post *ran a story on it in March 1954, the film was banned in Britain until 1968.*

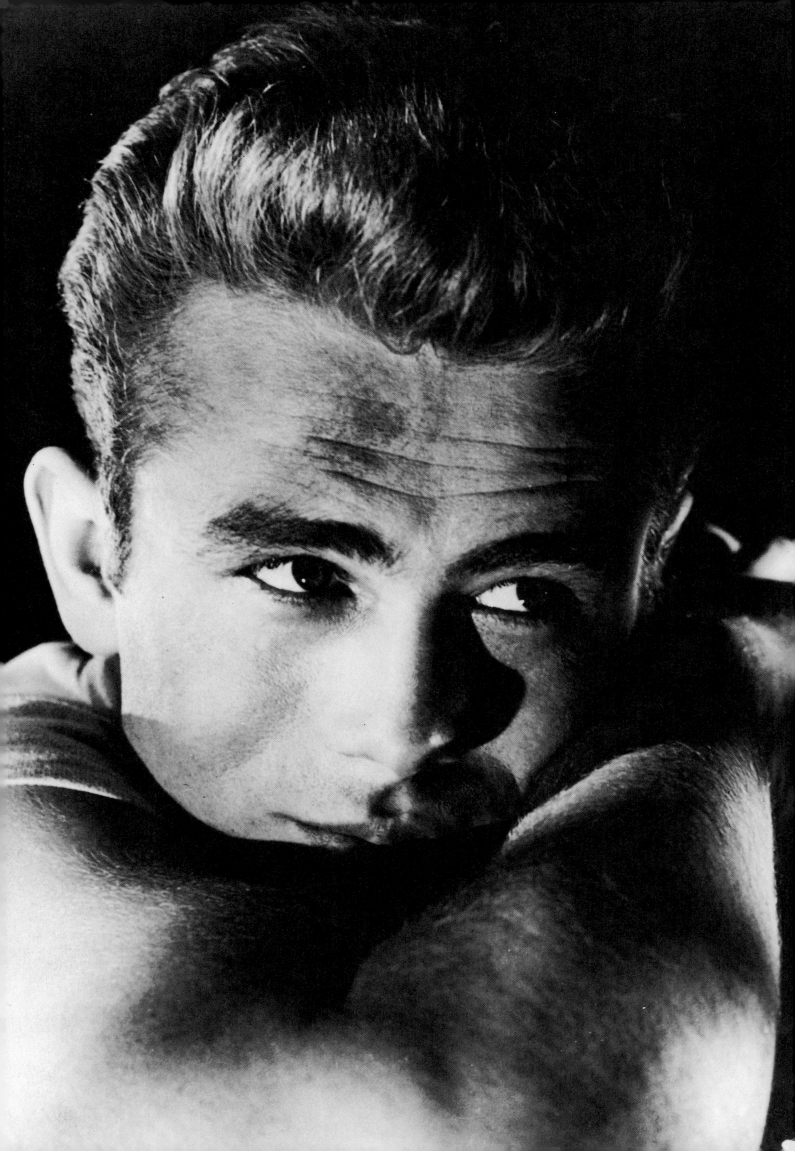

Rebel without a Cause

James Dean starred in only four films, but his good looks and tragically early death rapidly made him a cult figure. Picture Post *went James Dean crazy in* 1956. *All of the pictures were bought in.*

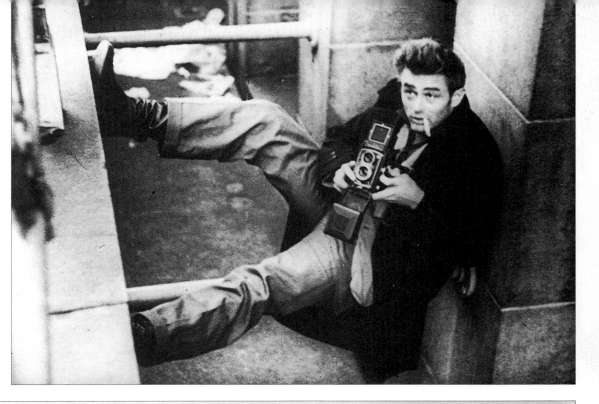

Burton and Taylor

Below: *The young Elizabeth Taylor, photographed in 1954 by Baron. A former child star, she had already made over twenty films.*

Right: *Richard Burton in a poignant shot – walking with his father in Wales, July 1953. His marriage to Taylor in 1963 helped set him on the path to international stardom.*

Images of Marilyn

Like James Dean, Marilyn Monroe was an idol whose premature death only enhanced her legend. Clockwise from top left: *with Joseph Cotten in* Niagara *(1952); an informal studio shot; in* Seven Year Itch *(1955);* Gentlemen Prefer Blondes *(1953).*

Left: *Tony Hancock, 1954;* above: Take
It From Here, *1953: Dick Bentley, June
Whitfield, Jimmy Edwards, Alma Cogan;*
right: *Arthur Askey and David Nixon,
1954;* below: Over to You, *1951: Richard
Murdoch, Kenneth Horne, Sam Costa.*

Famous faces from Fifties' TV. Clockwise
from top left: *Eamonn Andrews says 'This
is Your Life' to Diana Dors; Petula Clark
and her sister Barbara in* Pet's Parlour;
Jack Warner in Dixon of Dock Green;
*Richard Dimbleby filming in a lifeboat;
Benny Hill and his wig collection.*

Skiffle

Lonnie Donegan scored a big hit at the start of 1956 with skiffle, a sweetening of American blues and folk music little heard in Britain. His popularity made him a regular on TV shows like 6.5 Special.

Left to right: Dicky Bishop (guitar), Donny Wright (guitar) Lonnie Donegan (guitar), Nick Nicholls (drums, and Micky Ashman (bass).

Rock'n'roll arrives

Elvis Presley's first British hit was 'Heartbreak Hotel' in May 1956. 'Rock'n'roll arrives,' Picture Post proclaimed on their Elvis Presley cover; but without a Presley visit to the UK, the editors were forced to rely on bought-in shots – like these of Elvis in performance and (right) *on the set of* Love Me Tender, *his first film.*

'The Comets are Coming'

Bill Haley's visit to Britain in February 1957 was the first visit by a rock'n'roll star, and Picture Post *went along with the rest of the media in overkill. A good shot of the group on stage at the Dominion Theatre, on 7 February, was balanced, in typical* Picture Post *style, by a shot of the audience outside.*

The voice of Bermondsey

Five months before these shots were taken, Tommy Steele was an unknown ship's steward. But 'the Prince of Rock is a home boy really', said Picture Post – and their photographer went to Steele's Bermondsey home to prove it.

ACKNOWLEDGEMENTS

The majority of the pictures in this book are from the Hulton Picture Company and were taken by Picture Post *staff photographers. We have identified the work of individual* Picture Post *photographers where possible, but in some instances we have been unable to do so and we would like to apologise to anyone whose work has not been acknowledged below.*

Picture Post: *Maurice Ambler 67 (centre right), 121; John Chillingworth 61 (top), 110–11 (right), 112 (bottom left); Alex Dellow 94 (left & centre right), 134 (bottom); Gerti Deutsch 23 (bottom); George Douglas 78 (both), 79 (top); Malcolm Dunbar 96 (top right); Jack Esten 47, 119 (top); Daniel Farson 63 (all); Tim Gidal 12 (bottom); Zoltan Glass 29 (bottom right) and front cover picture of Laurence Olivier; Bert Hardy 6, 62 (bottom), 66 (top left), 73 (top right), 74–5 (all), 76–7, 80–1 (all), 83 (top right & bottom right), 88–9 (left), 97, 98–9, 105 (top), 110 (top left), 120 (bottom left) and front cover pictures of Frankie Howerd, Joan Collins and Noel Coward; Charles Hewitt 71, 79 (bottom), 82–3 (left), 84–5 (left), 86–7 (all), 95 (bottom), 110 (bottom left), 114 (left), 142 (all) and front cover picture of Peter Sellers; Thurston Hopkins 57 (bottom right), 66, 90–1, 103 (bottom), 118, 135 (bottom); Kurt Hutton 8, 14 (top right & both bottom), 15 (all), 23 (top right), 40, 44–5 (all), 58–9, 62 (top), 70 (top right), 114–5 (right), 120 (bottom right) and front and back cover pictures of Charlie Chaplin; Raymond Kleboe 50 (bottom), 56, 57 (both top & bottom left), 96 (bottom right), 128–9 (right); Leonard McCombe 38; Haywood Magee 1, 29 (centre right), 50 (top), 95 (top), 102, 103 (top), 105 (bottom), 112 (top left), 112–3 (right), 116–7, 119 (bottom), 127 (bottom right) and front cover pictures of Alma Cogan and Louis Armstrong; Felix Mann 22, 23 (top left), 29 (top right), 34 (bottom right), 35, 36 (top right), 37, 39 (top), 42–3 (all) and front cover picture of David Niven; Ronald Startup 70 (top left), 104.*

The remaining pictures are also from the Hulton Picture Company, with the exception of the following:
BBC Photograph Library: *16–7 (all), 89 (top right & bottom right), 92–3 (centre), 94 (top right & bottom right), 133 (both bottom), 134 (top), 135 (both top), 136–7.*
Bettmann Archive/Hulton Picture Company: *12 (top), 13, 26 (both), 55 (bottom), 124–5 and front cover picture of Humphrey Bogart.*
British Film Institute: *24–5 (both), 28 (bottom), 28–9 (top left), 72–3 (left), 108, 112 (centre left), 122 (top), 127 (centre & bottom left), 130 (top left) and front cover pictures of Marlon Brando and Sophia Loren.*
Kobal Collection: *18, 19, 32–3 (both), 54 (bottom), 55 (top), 73 (bottom right), 93 (right), 123, 126, 127 (top), 138 (top).*
London Features International: *2, 9, 27, 41, 92 (left), 130 (top right & bottom), 131, 138 (bottom), 139 and front cover pictures of Marlene Dietrich and Marilyn Monroe.*